T0010818

THE
Pacific Crest Trail

THE
Pacific Crest Trail

HIKING AMERICA'S WILDERNESS TRAIL

Foreword by **MARK LARABEE**   **BART SMITH**

Pacific Crest Trail
Association

RIZZOLI
NEW YORK

New York Paris London Milan

Foreword

ON A RECENT FALL WEEKENDER, A GROUP OF US WALKED into the Indian Heaven Wilderness in southern Washington. It's a favored place because of its proximity to our home in Oregon. When we're feeling the need to get away, it's easy to get to a trailhead and walk just a few miles to the junction of the Pacific Crest Trail (PCT), which sets us up for a nice hike to several pocket lakes surrounded by towering firs. The simple act of being there, even for a short walk and an overnight, can put a new lens on the week, sharpen the mind, and lift the spirit.

We in Portland are not alone in being within easy striking distance of the PCT. As the trail runs the length of California, Oregon, and Washington, weaving its way for 2,650 miles between Mexico and Canada, it's just a few hours at most from a handful of major cities. People in San Diego, Los Angeles, San Francisco, Portland, and Seattle—as well as countless smaller cities and

towns—have the trail at their back door. The PCT is easily accessible and incredibly remote all at once.

In its magnificent journey, the trail crosses the vast Mojave Desert, traverses the towering granite and high-alpine environs of the Sierra Nevada, meanders past the Cascade Volcanoes through lush forests, and finishes in the granite and wooded mountain wonderland of the North Cascades. The Indian Heaven Wilderness, southwest of Mount Adams, includes a high plateau with many meadows, large and small, as well as more than 150 lakes. The Yakama, Klickitat, Cascades, Wasco, Wishram, and Umatilla tribes recognized its gifts, gathering there annually to pick berries, hunt, and fish. The huckleberries are abundant in the fall and made for a great addition to our morning pancakes.

As we hiked out on a Sunday afternoon, the four of us paused for lunch in a grassy meadow. After we ate, we lay in the warm, dry grass, admiring the view, breathing in the delightful woodsy smell and listening to birds in a half-dazed state. Truth is, no one wanted to leave.

Beauty. Calm. Solitude. Peace. This is my PCT experience. In this place, in this state of mind, I find clarity that often eludes me in the frenetic pace of daily life. It's something I regularly yearn for from behind my keyboard.

As you thumb through Bart Smith's amazing photographs in this book, you will see why the Pacific Crest Trail, America's wilderness trail, is so highly loved and regarded. The trail crosses 48 federally protected wilderness areas—about half the trail runs through wilderness—each distinct in landscape and for the plants and animals that live there. These photographs capture the beauty of the trail in moments. They freeze these important places in time and tell a grand story in their own subtle way of our nation's dedication to preserving our best landscapes for future generations. These vast public lands and trails are an amazing gift, not only to those who will come after us, but also to ourselves.

This year we celebrate the 50th anniversary of the National Trails System Act, the 1968 law passed by Congress and signed by President Lyndon Johnson. The act designated the Pacific Crest and Appalachian Trails as the first two national scenic trails. Today, there are 11 national scenic trails and 19 national historic trails. These special trails, the best of the best, help protect the places they pass through as well as our historic and cultural heritage.

Enjoying these trails, rejoicing in their beauty and richness, is the easy part. Trails don't just happen. They take work, sweat equity, and dedication.

Without vigilance, they would likely be gone for good in the face of development pressure, resource extraction, and other ongoing threats to public-land preservation. Trails take love if they are to be sustained. It's no coincidence that the National Trails System Act calls out the necessity of volunteers and nonprofit groups such as the Pacific Crest Trail Association to be stewards of these great trails. The Congress of 1968 acknowledged the need for citizen caretakers with its near-unanimous passage of this landmark piece of legislation:

> *The Congress recognizes the valuable contributions that volunteers and private, nonprofit trail groups have made to the development and maintenance of the Nation's trails. In recognition of these contributions, it is further the purpose of this Act to encourage and assist volunteer citizen involvement in the planning, development, maintenance, and management, where appropriate.*

This prescient requirement bonds us as individuals and a community to the responsibility of taking care of the PCT and all the nation's trails. In partnership with our government, it is our civic and moral duty to pass on this heritage to generations that will come after us. They deserve no less.

What each of us takes away from our trips into the wild is both personal and, yet, universal. At the Pacific Crest Trail Association, we champion the cause of maintaining and protecting the trail and the experience it provides through strategic partnerships, volunteerism, activism, and individual and group achievements. By giving back to the trail that gives us so much, we pay it forward. I feel grateful for the gift the trail offers. I also understand how my individual contribution matters to this shared and honorable cause. There is simplicity and precision in that feeling, which brings clarity and peace.

MARK LARABEE
Associate Director of Communications and Marketing
Pacific Crest Trail Association

213

LIST OF PLATES

First published in the United States of America in 2019
by Rizzoli International Publications, Inc.
300 Park Avenue South
New York, NY 10010
www.rizzoliusa.com

© 2019 Rizzoli International Publications, Inc.
Photography © 2019 Bart Smith

Foreword Text: Mark Larabee
Project Editor: Candice Fehrman
Book Design: Susi Oberhelman

The mission of the Pacific Crest Trail Association is to protect,
preserve, and promote the Pacific Crest National Scenic Trail as a
world-class experience for hikers and equestrians, and for all the
values provided by wild and scenic lands. For more information,
please visit us at www.pcta.org.

2019 2020 2021 2022 / 10 9 8 7 6 5 4 3 2 1

Printed in China

ISBN-13: 978-0-8478-6451-5

Library of Congress Catalog Control Number: 2018954290